Original title:
The Porchlight's Promise

Copyright © 2025 Creative Arts Management OÜ
All rights reserved.

Author: Sophia Kingsley
ISBN HARDBACK: 978-1-80587-227-6
ISBN PAPERBACK: 978-1-80587-697-7

A Warm Glow Against the Chill

When night creeps in, we huddle near,
A flickering flame, our cozy sphere.
The cat's on guard, with eyes aglow,
While we debate if cats are in the know.

The door creaks loud, we laugh and say,
It's just the ghosts wanting to play.
With popcorn bowls and jokes in tow,
We make our own warmth, come ice or snow.

Comfort in the Twilight

The twilight calls, we settle down,
With pillows fluffy, oh what a crown!
A cup in hand, let laughter flow,
Let's reminisce on where we'll go.

The neighbors shout, does someone even care?
We toss them snacks, just to be fair.
A comet zooms, we throw our hats,
Who knew the nights invited such chats?

Illuminate the Forgotten Path

The garden path, once lost in weeds,
Now sparkles bright, fulfilling needs.
We dared to twirl, through shadows long,
As crickets chirp their night-time song.

But watch your step, there's gnomes about,
They've fortified the route, no doubt.
As fairy lights on branches sway,
We tripped and laughed all night away.

Together Under a Blaze of Stars

Beneath the sky, we lie in bliss,
A galaxy sparked, what did we miss?
We count the stars, issue a dare,
Can we catch one? Let's just declare!

We share our dreams, with hiccups too,
While aiming for that cosmic view.
With goofy grins and eyes so wide,
This is where our fears abide.

The Glow of Morning Wishes

In the dawn of a sleepy town,
The rooster crows, but I just frown.
Coffee spills, a messy start,
Yet laughter cheers a heavy heart.

Bacon sizzles, a smoky song,
Cats run wild, they can't be wrong.
Slip on socks, oh where's that shoe?
A dance of chaos, just a day or two.

Light's Gentle Touch on Heartstrings

A flicker of warmth on a chilly night,
My neighbor's dog claims the porch light bright.
With snacks in hand, we gather 'round,
To share our tales of joy unbound.

The cat, however, steals the show,
Dressed in a tutu, oh what a glow!
We roll with laughter, our worries flee,
As stories twine like yarn on a spree.

A Beacon of Belonging

Under the stars, we spin our dreams,
Ah, but first, let's plot our ice cream schemes!
With sprinkles, fudge, and cherry on top,
Our smiles shine brighter, we just can't stop.

Forget the phones, it's laughter's reign,
As we toss popcorn in the rain.
A world where all our quirks align,
Holding hands, we sip on sunshine wine.

Resilience Wrapped in Warmth

A cozy blanket, a wobbly chair,
We share our wisdom while breathing air.
With bold tales of mishaps and spills,
We chase the night with our giggles and thrills.

As twilight dances, shadows play,
Our porchlight hums a joy today.
With every promise of warmth and cheer,
In every chuckle, our hearts draw near.

Reflections of Hope in Glowing Warmth

Beneath the glow of evening's cheer,
The cat pounces on shadows near.
With every leap it claims the night,
As bugs all buzz in dim delight.

The neighbors peek with curious eyes,
Wondering what's the feline's prize.
With every tumble and each fall,
The porchlight laughs at it all!

A Flame's Whisper in the Stillness

Crisp packets rustle like gossiping ghosts,
As shadows dance, they love to boast.
The light flickers, like a teasing wink,
Is that a raccoon? I really think!

He approaches, in search of a snack,
Then trips on a toy and does a backtrack.
Amidst the chaos, the light holds sway,
Keeps us laughing, come what may!

The Light That Never Fades

Two old friends swap tales on the stoop,
As crickets join the fun, what a troupe!
With laughter echoing, the night's a stage,
Each story shared, another age.

The light above hums, a soft old tune,
Turning the mundane into a festoon.
When evening falls and worries creep,
The light retains secrets we shall keep.

Sheltered by a Radiant Glow

A weary owl perches with pride,
Rolling its eyes, like it wants to hide.
The porchlight dances, casting spells,
On squirrels that think they're circusells.

Each blunder met with guffaws and spins,
Their antics match the light's bright grins.
In this cozy glow, joy takes flight,
While the whole world fades into the night.

Guiding Gleam at Dusk

In the evening as cats prance,
You stumble on your own two pants.
The glow reveals the bugs a-fly,
Waving hands and cats nearby.

Your snacks are safe, just not your hair,
As moths declare their party flair.
A light that winks, a beacon bright,
As laughter echoes through the night.

Whispering Light Beyond the Threshold

A glow emerges, soft and strange,
It pulls you close to dance and change.
The shadows giggle, slip, and sway,
While crickets join the grand ballet.

With every step, a squeak, a squawk,
A shuffled step, a wibbly walk.
Yet through the chaos, light remains,
As every clumsy bump explains.

Shadows Dance in the Glow

A flickering flit, the shadows prance,
In the light, they spin and dance.
Each movement brings a chuckle near,
As dread makes way for hearty cheer.

The cat leaps high, the dog does twirl,
A saucy bug makes his grand whirl.
With every laugh, and each mistake,
The bright light holds, for fun's own sake.

Beacon of Hope from Afar

From a distance, the light shines wide,
It beckons more than just your pride.
A snack awaits, but so does fate,
As you trip again, it's never late.

A beacon calls, now far, now near,
While unexpected guests draw near.
In shadows wild, you twirl and sway,
With warmth of laughter leading the way.

The Glistening Path to Tomorrow

In the glow of a bulb, we stake our claim,
Waiting for adventures that never seem lame.
With dreams in our pockets, we dance and we sway,
Tripping on wishes that chase us all day.

So here on the porch, we plot and we scheme,
Building our castles out of soft ice cream.
Tomorrow will come with a wink and a grin,
As we chase fireflies, let the fun begin!

Safe Harbor in the Night's Embrace

Under the stars, with a snack in one hand,
We tell silly stories, as only friends can.
The night is our ship, and we're sailing away,
To a place where there's laughter and games always play.

With blankets like sails, we drift on our dreams,
Finding treasures in rumpled old jeans.
Each joke that we tell spins a star in the sky,
In the safe harbor of laughter, we always fly high.

The Light That Holds Memories Tight

The porch light flickers with tales of our youth,
Of mix-ups in baking and wild sizes of tooth.
The glow wraps around us like a soft, warm hug,
While we giggle and tease and share secrets to plug.

We map out our past like a treasure with flair,
From slip-ups to giggles, we venture everywhere.
Each laugh like a firework, bursts bright in the night,
Hold fast to those memories, they make chaos feel right.

Heartbeats Beneath the Glow

With shadows dancing like puppets on strings,
We leap over dreams, shake off the bad things.
The porchlight above hums a tune in our hearts,
As we plot our escape with some very odd charts.

Whispers of laughter and stories from days,
Mix with the fireflies in a whimsical blaze.
Each moment a treasure, a masterpiece bright,
Underneath all the giggles, we're soaring in flight.

Warmth on a Winter's Eve

A bulb flickers, like a wink,
Inviting smiles, don't you think?
Cold nips at noses, yet we stand,
With cocoa cups and laughs unplanned.

Snowflakes dance in their sparkling glee,
As we swap stories, just you and me.
The porchlight glows, a beacon bright,
In this cozy glow, all feels just right.

Illuminated Path of Dreams

Shoes left outside in the snow's embrace,
The porchlight shouts, "Join the warm space!"
Trip on the rug, but we won't complain,
Because laughter bubbles like joy in champagne.

A dog sniffs around for the shiniest snack,
While shadows dance on the door's creaky track.
With every chuckle, the night draws in,
Under this beacon, the fun can't thin.

A Lantern's Embrace

The lantern swings, a gentle tease,
Chasing moths like whispering breeze.
With every giggle, the night feels bold,
As we brave the winter, hand in hand, so cold.

Kittens pounce as if it's a game,
The porchlight flickers, we call each name.
Every face shines, a tapestry bright,
In the glow of the lantern, all is all right.

Where Hearts Find Their Way

Under a starry, twinkling sky,
The porch invites, with laughter nigh.
Come, gather round, share tales of cheer,
While the porchlight hums, "No need to fear!"

A pot of stew keeps spirits alight,
As we trade stories well into the night.
The glow of joy, it reaches afar,
In this warm embrace, we are all stars.

A Sentinel of Solace

In the glow of night, I see
An odd cat grinning at me.
He swears he guards my dreams so bright,
But snores louder than my porch light.

The neighbors think I'm quite a sight,
Dancing with shadows, feeling light.
But it's not just the wine I sip,
It's the moon's laughter—a joyful trip.

Bugs join the bash, a bizarre crew,
Doing a jig, all askew.
They buzz along, in funny tune,
While I sway gently beneath the moon.

So here I sit, my secret throne,
With critters and bugs, I'm never alone.
For solace lives in every beam,
Light your laughter, chase your dream.

Flickering Flames of Reassurance

A candle flickers, sparks a thought,
Does it think it knows a lot?
While I sit with my herbal tea,
It's got a dimmer, just like me.

The shadows dance, a silly sight,
That's Bob, the bug, in full flight.
He thinks he's brave, a tiny knight,
But I'm sure he's lost the fight!

The breeze sings songs of laughter shared,
As I strum my memories, none compared.
The night's a stage, a quirky play,
With bugs as stars, they steal the day.

So come and join this lively crew,
With chuckles spilling, a joke or two.
For in this glow, we find delight,
As flickers banish all the fright.

The Soft Call of Evening Light

The dusk blows in, the sun's farewell,
And out from shadows, our laughter swells.
A light so soft, it whispers clear,
Come sit a spell, let's share a beer!

The porch swing creaks, an old refrain,
It sways with tales of joy and pain.
Yet here we laugh, at life's delight,
By this soft glow, all feels just right.

A grandpa's joke springs from his chair,
While my dog dreams of a game of air.
The stars above are winking bright,
In this mellow glow, all feels just right.

So gather round, let stories fly,
And trust the dusk, never ask why.
For in this warmth, our hearts unite,
In the soothing call of evening light.

Lanterns Leading Us Home

With lanterns bright, we roam the street,
Chasing stray cats, on tiny feet.
They lead us 'round, wild and free,
Each twist and turn, a joyful spree.

The glow of lights, a silly chase,
As friends become a vibrant frame.
We tumble forth, with laughter loud,
Feeling like the best of a crowd.

Bugs join the band with a little hum,
As we all sway to the evening drum.
This happy mix, our playful dome,
In the lantern light, we find our home.

So here's to nights of whimsical cheer,
To lanterns bright and friends so dear.
For in this dance, we're never alone,
As light leads laughter, guiding us home.

Guardians of the Night

When nighttime creeps with silly grins,
The raccoons plan their little sins.
They dance around like clumsy fools,
Under the light, breaking all the rules.

My dog, the watchman, barks and leaps,
As shadows come from where laughter seeps.
He guards the yard with serious flair,
While cats just yawn, not a care to spare.

A stray cat saunters, all full of sass,
Beneath the glow, she struts with class.
She swears she owns this moonlit space,
While I just chuckle at her funny grace.

Oh, night falls down, with giggles loud,
As crickets chirp and shadows crowd.
In silly antics and funny sights,
We find our joy on these cozy nights.

Where Comfort Finds Its Place

In cushions soft and laughter bright,
The sofa holds its bustling night.
Popcorn flies amidst the fun,
While silly faces bump and run.

The cat claims pride on the warm seat,
While kids debate on snack to eat.
With giggles shared and tales spun,
This cozy spot, oh, it weighs a ton.

A blanket fort, the perfect hide,
With secret giggles kept inside.
We plot adventures, wild and grand,
Where fun is made, and snacks are planned.

The night rolls on with joyful cheer,
In this haven, we've nothing to fear.
For in these moments, side by side,
We find our comfort, our laughter, our pride.

Beneath the Watchful Glow

Under a glow that flickers bright,
The bugs join in the dance at night.
With buzzing tunes and little lights,
They flaunt their moves, oh what a sight!

The garden's full of misplaced socks,
And gnomes who laugh, hiding in flocks.
They tell tall tales while sipping dew,
As fireflies join in, a merry crew.

A neighbor sneaks with bags of chips,
While kids embark on secret trips.
The glow reveals their silly schemes,
As laughter tints our midnight dreams.

With shadows dancing, spirits high,
We sing our songs beneath the sky.
In every flicker, a story's spun,
This wacky night, oh, what fun we've won!

Lanterns Guide Our Way

With lanterns swinging in the breeze,
Each step we take stirs up the leaves.
Ghost stories told with hesitant grins,
As shadows loom and the laughter spins.

The lanterns flicker; we fear a fright,
But giggles take flight in the soft twilight.
We stumble through patches of wild blooms,
Swatting away imaginary grooms.

Each light a beacon, our big parade,
As we craft mischief, unafraid.
With every corner, a silly scare,
We find the fun lurking everywhere.

So let the lanterns shine so bright,
As we chase the giggles through endless night.
In every glow and shadow's play,
Forever kids, come what may!

Glow of Hope

In the dusk, a light does gleam,
Bugs swarm by like a crazy dream.
I trip on stairs, I spill my tea,
The neighbors laugh, they take a pea.

The dog can't find a place to sit,
He barks at shadows, gives a fit.
A spider weaves a web so grand,
I wave it off with a clumsy hand.

A cat appears and claims the chair,
My snack now gone without a care.
The stars are bright, but not my luck,
As I find out I've lost my sock.

Yet in this chaos, joy is found,
In laughter's echo, we're all bound.
For every stumble, every blight,
We'll dance around this quirky light.

Beacon in the Twilight

Twilight falls as I juggle plates,
A dance with dinner, oh, such fates!
A flicker glows, it's not a fire,
Just my cooking, I'm such a liar.

A raccoon peeks from the bushes wide,
He steals my snacks; he can't abide.
I chase him off with a plastic fork,
He laughs and rolls, my nightly dork.

The light shows up my garden's fail,
Weeds flaunt colors, oh, the trail!
I trip and land on potato sacks,
My glow of hope? It's all just cracks.

But, hey, this madness feels just right,
As laughter dances in the night.
With each odd sight, I find my glee,
This wacky world is joyfully me.

Whispered Wishes Under Stars

Under the stars, wishes take flight,
I wish for cash, but get a fright.
The moon's in on it, playing tricks,
My thoughts go wild like playful flicks.

A shooting star zooms past with flair,
I duck and dodge, it's quite unfair.
The wishes I make sound absurd and loud,
Hoping for wise, I end up proud.

My friend yells, "Check that odd-shaped cloud!"
A dolphin shape, it doesn't quite wow.
In whispers soft, we tell our dreams,
With giggles shared, nothing's as it seems.

Yet when the dawn colors the sky,
We pack our hopes like a lullaby.
For every laugh and silly jest,
We find our peace, it's truly blessed.

Embrace of the Evening Light

Evening calls with a glow so warm,
I bring out snacks to ignite the charm.
A breeze comes in, it flips my hat,
The strawberries roll, where's a cat?

Bug bites nibble on my skin,
The night is sweet, despite the din.
Yet here I stand, a sight, indeed,
With chips on my face, I'm in the lead.

My friend arrives, with ice cream too,
We're two hot messes, it's quite the brew.
The light above is dim and sweet,
Reflecting mischief in our fleet.

But in this glow, we laugh and sway,
Embracing all, come what may.
For in the end, it's simple and true,
The fun we share outshines the blue.

Stories Illuminated by Twilight

When the sun dips low, the tales arise,
Of squirrels in capes and pizza pies.
The moon winks bright, like a playful tease,
While crickets debate the best types of cheese.

Old chairs creak loud, sharing secrets sly,
Of mishaps and laughter that never die.
With a wink and a grin, shadows dance,
As fireflies flirt, like they're in a romance.

The Haven of Dimming Lumens

In this cozy nook, the glow is dim,
Where cats plan heists on a lonely whim.
A lamp flickers like it's had too much wine,
While toast pops up like it's drawing a line.

Stories swirl like the dust in the air,
Of socks gone missing and old armchair flair.
With a chuckle and sigh, we bask in delight,
In this haven of glow, everything feels right.

A Trusting Flame in Solitude

A candle flickers, casting strange shapes,
Like dancing llamas in funny capes.
The shadows giggle as they beam and glide,
While the potted plant decides to hide.

Lonely but bright, it whispers to me,
"Let's throw a party, just wait and see!"
With popcorn and laughs, memories ignite,
A warm, goofy glow fills the quiet night.

Echoes of Light

The glow of the bulb hums a bright tune,
As bugs plot to crash the disco moon.
With laughter that bounces off walls of old,
And stories retold of adventures bold.

The night drips with dreams, quirky and loud,
As the echoes of fun gather 'round the crowd.
Each glow a reminder of moments we shared,
Witty banter and laughter, no one is spared.

A Return to Love

With a sprinkle of light and a dash from the stars,
We gather 'round memories held under jars.
Old wooden chairs that creak with each word,
As laughter spills out, both joyful and heard.

Whimsical glow lights up cheeks full of joy,
As friends reminisce of each silly ploy.
In this gentle light, love circles around,
Transforming the night into laughter unbound.

Guiding Beacon

In the night, a bulb does glow,
A guiding light for all below.
Cats do twirl in moonlit dance,
While humans trip in their own pants.

With snacks in hand and friends at play,
We laugh at mishaps on display.
Neighbors peek from curtains wide,
As we stumble like stars that glide.

Lanterns of Reminiscence

Before the dawn, we gather near,
With tales of woe, we shed a tear.
A lantern flickers, it starts to sway,
It plays the soundtrack of our day.

Old socks and stories fill the air,
Was that a ghost? Oh, do we dare?
Ghosts of choices made in jest,
Tonight's our chance to outshine the rest.

Shadows and Dreams

Shadows dance beneath the moon,
A sly raccoon sings a tune.
We share our dreams with loud delight,
While our shoes are chewed by the night.

Hopscotch games on golden grass,
As fireflies wink and moments pass.
Who knew a porch could be so grand?
With laughter echoing through the land.

Safe Haven at Dusk

As daylight fades, we gather tight,
A haven found in fading light.
With jokes so bad they start to sting,
We cheer like it's a grand old thing.

Pet dogs rolling, cats in sight,
A turtle wins a race tonight.
In this safe space, our troubles flee,
As we sip tea and let life be.

Guiding Flame in the Night

A flicker bright invites me in,
Where shadows leap and giggles spin.
The cats parade, like tiny queens,
While bugs collide in silly scenes.

The light's a beacon, no need to fret,
I'll dodge the weeds, and I won't forget.
As I tiptoe through the garden maze,
In search of snacks, and midnight praise.

I hear a rustle, a suspicious sound,
Is that a ghost, or just the hound?
No time for fright, let's make it fun,
With ghostly laughs, till day is done.

So here's to lights that guide our way,
In a world where mischief loves to play.
With every glimmer, a chuckle grows,
In the night's embrace, joy overflows.

A Ray of Trust Amidst the Gloom

In shadows deep, trust takes a seat,
A flicker shines, it can't be beat.
The raccoons gather, in secret clouts,
While I'm outsmarted, by all the scouts.

With every blink of this tiny light,
I step with caution, avoiding fright.
Is that a bat, or just my hat?
More laughs arise from this friendly spat.

In every corner of the dark,
A chance for giggles, a hall of larks.
I'm off to find some late-night snacks,
In a world where humor never lacks.

So here's to trust in the dark of night,
Where laughter blooms, and fear takes flight.
Beneath the glow, let worries cease,
In this silly dance, may we find peace.

Hushed Promises in the Twilight

In the twilight's soft embrace,
Promises linger, we can't disgrace.
The porchlight winks, a playful tease,
While moths engage in a dance of sneeze.

With every glow, the stories spin,
Of critters plotting, where to begin.
A chair-rock's tune, like whispers shared,
Of adventures there, that we once dared.

The shadows stretch, with cheeky grins,
While I hunt for the snacks, where are the chips?
This giggling orb, brings us delight,
In hush and laughter, a crazy night.

So here's to twilight's gentle charm,
When laughter shields us, safe from harm.
In hushed tones, our friendship thrives,
In every glow, our spirit jives.

Glimmering Dreams at Day's End

At day's end, dreams start to twirl,
In the glow of light, mischief will unfurl.
Chasing shadows, what can they do?
Join in the laugh, as the night renews.

Beneath the stars, the antics rise,
Where every flicker wears a disguise.
The socks are lost, the cats run wild,
In this chaotic carnival, I'm a child.

As the moon giggles, a dance we hold,
With secrets exchanged, like treasures of gold.
A toast to laughs, with friends so dear,
In gleaming dreams, we cast off fear.

So when the light begins to glow,
Remember to let your laughter flow.
With every spark, new dreams ascend,
In the night's embrace, all worries bend.

Refuge in the Glow

In the night I seek a beam,
A flicker bright, a gentle theme.
Bugs buzzing round in clumsy dance,
They crash and bounce, they take their chance.

The neighbor's cat, a curious spy,
With whispers soft, and glances sly.
I wave to her, she flicks her tail,
As if to say, 'Did you just fail?'

A snack awaits, I see it gleam,
Chips in hand, I munch and dream.
The porch, my throne, my royal seat,
With crumbs to spare, it can't be beat.

Laughter rolls with easy grace,
As friends drop by, we share this space.
Amidst the glow, jokes take their flight,
In this warm land, all feels just right.

A Light in the Gloom

Through the dark, a glimmer sings,
A humble lamp, with hefty wings.
It guides me home, with humorous flair,
Even shadows chuckle, light in the air.

That old chair creaks, a friend in need,
It tells its tales, making me heed.
The wind joins in, a comedic guest,
Tickling my hair, an unexpected jest.

Fireflies join, a flashing jest,
Competing bright, they try their best.
I sip my drink, and giggle low,
As these little lights put on a show.

In this space where laughter grows,
With laughter bold, and friendship flows.
A light in gloom, we bask and sway,
As silly moments dance and play.

The End of the Day's Wander

As daylight ends, my humor's swell,
The sky blushes, it knows me well.
A porch so cozy, my bum finds rest,
While the crickets chirp, they host a fest.

Neighbors shout, their voices cheer,
From across the street, it's good to hear.
Stories shared, with giggles tight,
While the universe glows, just right.

A squirrel frolics, with nuts to stash,
He looks like he's ready for a mad dash.
I raise my glass, to toast this crew,
It's not just me, they're nuts too!

In twilight's grip, we lie back and jest,
The day has faded, we're feeling blessed.
With laughter soft, we wrap the night,
In this tender glow, all feels just right.

Hope's Gentle Flame

A glow appears, just like a dream,
Chasing away the night's loud scream.
With each flicker, a grin does grow,
As I sip my soda, and start the show.

Beneath the stars, my friends take stage,
Each telling tales, full of rage.
The garden gnome, a silent judge,
As to his humor, we all must budge.

My chair squeaks loud, a funny sound,
As I lean back, my arms unbound.
Laughter erupts with tales retold,
In this moonlit magic, we bravely uphold.

So cheers to nights, when we all huddle near,
In the glow of joy, life's mysteries clear.
Hope's gentle flame lights up our way,
As we laugh into the breezy sway.

Memory's Light at Dusk

In the yard, the cat's a spy,
Stalking shadows, oh so sly.
A tattered chair, my throne of kings,
As laughter bounces, the nightbird sings.

The fireflies dance, a twinkling crew,
I swear they wink—do you see it too?
My old dog snores, dreams of a chase,
While I conquer worlds from this cozy place.

An ice cream truck, its jingle neat,
But I'm too full of snack-time treats.
The neighbors argue—who's lawn's the best?
While I recline, oh, this is the quest!

With goofy grins and playful shouts,
We spin our tales without any doubts.
Memory's light flickers, never dies,
Turning our dusk into comedy skies.

Homeward Bound by Soft Light

The moon's a lamp, and I'm the moth,
Can't help but laugh, I'm just a sloth.
Wobbling home on silly feet,
Tripping over pumpkins—my nighttime treat!

The porch swings beckon, creaking low,
With ghostly tales that come and go.
A cat's meow, a ghostly flare,
Let's spin a yarn from this cozy chair.

My socks mismatched, I've lost the fight,
But watch me dance in the moonlight!
Neighbors peek through curtains tight,
But I just twirl, what a funny sight!

A hot dog splat, toppings everywhere,
With ketchup dreams in big despair.
We lift our cups, toast to the night,
In this silly chaos, oh what a delight!

The Flame That Unites Us

In the backyard, with sizzling snacks,
We roast marshmallows, dodging the flaks.
A shadow jumps—was that a raccoon?
Or my brother trying to make a moon?

Laughter erupts, chips fly free,
Tangled in tales as deep as the sea.
The sun drops low, the flame gets bright,
My sister's jokes? Pure comedy fright!

We poke at the fire, stir up some ash,
While recounting tales of our childhood crash.
The sparks shoot out—a fiery cheer,
Like our hearts, it flickers year after year.

So here's to the nights we cozy and share,
Let's roast our fears over this flare.
Raucous and reckless, in laughter we trust,
Together we stand, in fire and dust.

Glimmers of Love on Starlit Nights

Under the stars, a blanket spread,
Popcorn's flying, no one's fed.
We howl at the moon, like wise old owls,
Sharing secrets, sweet little growls.

Sneaky cupcakes hid in the grass,
As our giggles echo, we let them pass.
A playful tug-of-war with a shoe,
Laughter spills like morning dew.

Tales of ghosts that dance with flair,
While Dad snores, not a single care.
The dog joins in, a curious bark,
Oh what a circus, under the park!

With glimmers of love on this fine night,
Our silly moments take rapid flight.
Bonded in laughter, we dream and we play,
In this starry haven, forever we stay.

The Light That Waits

In a glow that flickers bright,
Cats convene for a midnight bite.
Neighbors yell, 'Is that a raccoon?'
While I chase shadows, howling at the moon.

A sandwich left, a daring snack,
On the porch, I'll stage my attack.
But what's that rustling, could it be?
A squirrel plotting a heist on me?

With each passing car, my spirits rise,
Their headlights dancing like fireflies.
I wave to the ghosts of my late-night crew,
Who all agree, the food's getting due.

So here I stand, weathered and frail,
Guarding my sandwich with a bright, goofy wail.
Under the stars, I'll wait and jest,
For the light that waits is truly the best.

Horizons of Comfort

Under bright skies, with lazy flair,
Chairs rock silently, catching the air.
Ice cream drips down, a sticky affair,
As I gaze at clouds, my mind trips with care.

The neighbor's dog starts a woofing spree,
As I laugh with a heart full of glee.
A raccoon on my table, bold and spry,
Waves with a paw and steals a fry.

We make small bets on who will win,
Will it be the dog or the raccoon kin?
A showdown brewing in this porch light glow,
Comfort found where the silly winds blow.

As night drapes its cloak of starlit schemes,
I'll sit on my porch and follow my dreams.
With laughter echoing far and wide,
This horizon of comfort, my trusty guide.

Vigil of the Night Watch

At dusk, I take my favored chair,
On duty now, with not a care.
A mug of coffee stains my shirt,
As I scan the dark for mischief's flirt.

The bugs come dancing, oh what a show,
They twirl and spin like they're in a row.
But watch out, friends, the cats are near,
With eyes aglow, they'll stalk without fear.

A burglar? Nay, just the mailman's step,
Bringing me news that I won't intercept.
I sit and ponder the night's quirky charms,
As crickets croon their soothing psalms.

My watch is simple, my post is clear,
Guarding the porch from shadows near.
With chuckles loud and worries slight,
In my vigilant chair, I greet the night.

The Lure of Luminescence

A bulb that buzzes, an alluring sight,
Bugs zoom in for a dance, what a fright!
They crash like pilots with no flight plan,
While I sip old soda from a rusty can.

The glow draws in the neighbors' gaze,
As I tell tales in my silliest ways.
A daredevil moth tries to claim my stew,
While I shout, 'Hey buddy, it's not meant for you!'

With every flicker, my heart takes flight,
In the warm embrace of the glowing night.
Comrades gather, under starry schemes,
Where laughter echoes and everybody beams.

So here's to the moments we foolishly find,
With beams of light that are sweet and kind.
In this dance of life, with spirits bright,
We're lured together in the lure of light.

Illumination at Journey's End

A beacon bright with quirky glee,
It guides the lost like a carnival spree.
Waving hello to the folks that roam,
It whispers, 'You're almost home!'

Bugs might dance in the flickering light,
But we've got snacks and laughter tonight.
With every tale, laughter goes around,
Our wise advice? Never wear a clown's crown!

The neighbor's cat struts like a king,
Proud of the chaos that night can bring.
With glow-in-the-dark balloons in the air,
We summon the moon, if it dares to care!

So we raise a toast to strange delights,
To glowing secrets and silly frights.
For at this end, what matters most,
Is joy, and laughter, and a friendly roast!

Remnants of Radiance

Flickering lights and crumbs of pie,
Old tales of woe that make us sigh.
The chair creaks loud in the evening hush,
While we argue if 'tis art or just mush.

Grandma's stories never lose their glow,
Especially when retold with a 'whoa!'
The socks mismatched in a vibrant spree,
Are just the start of this wild jubilee!

With laughter ringing from dusk till dawn,
We dance and giggle, forgetting the yawn.
And in this haven, life's quirks we embrace,
Draped in twilight, each smile finds its place.

So, gather round in this warm embrace,
Where even the shadows have a funny face.
The past may fade, but here comes the fun,
Under the glow of what's left undone!

Cradle of Contemplation

A porch so wide, where thoughts take flight,
Chasing fireflies into the night.
With lemonade spills and a lazy sigh,
We ponder life while the crickets cry.

With socks on hands, we debate the stars,
Who placed them there? Was it aliens or cars?
A cosmic riddle wrapped in our dreams,
We giggle and guffaw at our silly schemes.

The old dog snores like a rusty engine,
While we argue over last weekend's binge-in.
In the cradle of dark, wisdom might sprout,
But mostly it's laughter, without a doubt!

So pull up a chair in this thoughtful glow,
We'll laugh at life and its quirky show.
For while we ponder, the night drifts on,
In this cradle, we'll dance till dawn!

Serenity's Glow

A porch swing creaks like a wise old sage,
With laughter spilling from every page.
The stars above join in the fun,
Twinkling brightly, one by one.

The dogs chase shadows, like experts so sly,
While old folks sip tea and kids just fly.
With jokes that linger and stories that grow,
Life's secrets unfold in serenity's glow.

The neighbor's music is offbeat and loud,
Yet here we sway, an unruly crowd.
With every mishap, a hearty cheer,
Our nighttime revelry turns into a seer.

So let's toast to those moments so bright,
Where laughter and dreams take formal flight.
In this swirl of friends, we'll brightly glow,
For happiness thrives where love is aglow!

Illumination of Forgotten Roads

A flicker in the night, it gleams,
Chasing away my wildest dreams.
I trip over the garden gnome,
Who's here when I'm too far from home.

With snacks in hand, I greet the light,
"What's cooking?" I ask, with delight.
The porch has never been so bold,
It whispers secrets, and tales unfold.

Raindrops dance upon the roof,
I laugh, "Is that a warming proof?"
As shadows leap and quietly mock,
Even my socks feel like a rock!

To every wanderer, take heed,
The glow must always lead our creed.
With every laugh, and every cheer,
The dim-lit world feels much more clear.

The Light That Welcomes All

Come one, come all, the light does say,
Grab a snack, and let's laugh today!
The welcome mat has seen its share,
Of friends, old tales, and quirky flair.

Tommy slipped, and oh, what a sight!
He danced like a chicken in moonlight.
The lamp just chuckled, it knows too well,
How mixing joy can break the swell.

The dog is staring, quite perplexed,
Why humans gather, it's so vexed.
But then it spots a crumbly treat,
And joins the fun with clumsy feet.

So here we are, with lanterns bright,
We forge ahead, to dazzle the night.
In every twinkle, in every call,
Find joy abounding; it welcomes all!

Evening's Embrace of Assurance

As daylight fades, we find our way,
The porchlight glows, it wants to play.
A moth dances, quite out of tune,
While crickets serenade the moon.

"Is that a ghost?" I gasp in jest,
But really it's just my old zest.
The shadows tease, but here I stand,
A soda pop in one hand.

At dusk, chuckles fill the air,
With every glance, a silly stare.
We swap tall tales and crazy dreams,
While laughter echoes in vibrant beams.

So here we sit, with thoughts amiss,
Embraced by light, there's bliss in this.
Let every goof bring us some cheer,
As evening hugs, we're all sincere!

Flickers of Hope Among Shadows

A cozy nook under starry skies,
Where quirks emerge and laughter flies.
The light flickers with a knowing grin,
While shadows sigh, "Let the fun begin!"

"Did you hear that?" laughs fill the dark,
"It's just the fridge making its spark!"
As we giggle, a puppy rolls,
With each tumble, he steals our souls.

Magic blends with playful jest,
In this glow, we feel our best.
With stories wiggling and pranks inside,
The porchlight shines with boundless pride.

So come on by, let's dance a while,
In the warmth, let every heart smile.
For flickers of hope are found tonight,
Among the fun, we find our light.

Whispers of Radiance at Sundown

As twilight falls and shadows dance,
I trip on shoes, not quite by chance.
The lawn gnomes giggle, what a sight,
My dance with darkness, oh what a fright!

Glowbugs hum a merry tune,
I swear they're laughing at the moon.
With each misstep, my friends just cheer,
Who knew the night could bring such fear?

A swing takes flight, I'm soaring high,
But find my snack is waving goodbye.
Burgers burn while I try to sing,
In this wild circus, I'm the king!

So let the laughter light our way,
In these silly games, we'll forever play.
For every stumble, for every blink,
In our shared moments, we'll never sink.

Enchantment in the Ember's Glow

Around the fire, we toast marshmallows,
While Larry claims he can juggle shadows.
One goes left, the other goes right,
A campfire circus, oh what a sight!

If stories were gold, ours would be rich,
But who took a bite of my favorite sandwich?
The dogs all stare with wide-open eyes,
As we spin wild tales wrapped in lies.

Flames flicker, casting quirky shapes,
We talk of monsters and colorful tapes.
With every crackle, the laughter flows,
In this glow of friendship, our joy only grows.

So raise a toast to the silly night,
Where laughter sparkles like stars in flight.
In this whimsical glow, let's find the cheer,
With every smile, we hold each other near.

The Light of Togetherness

Underneath the old oak tree,
A gathering of friends, just you and me.
We set for fun with games and snacks,
And watch as squirrels conduct playful attacks.

A pie plate swings, a frisbee, too,
I aim for clouds, but hit a shoe.
With each missed throw, our laughter swells,
Even the neighbors play along—oh well!

The stars grow bright; a competition begins,
Who can tell the best of all the sins?
Mine's about a cat who wore a hat,
And danced with birds; can you beat that?

So come and join this cheerful crew,
Our laughter echoes, the joy feels new.
In this moment, our hearts all shine,
Together we create, a bond divine.

A Glimpse Beyond the Darkness

In the depth of night, a faint flicker,
Uncle Joe's jokes just couldn't be thicker.
He claims he's wise, but it's hard to see,
When his belly laughs sound like a bumblebee.

The dogs start barking, join the fray,
As Aunt Sue tells tales in her quirky way.
Her stories twist and turn like a spin,
We're laughing so hard, it's a wild win!

A plush raccoon steals my favorite hat,
I chase him around—and just like that!
I trip on a garden gnome so brave,
Who knew we'd need a rescue wave?

So here's to the nights where the dark is bright,
With laughter ringing, everything feels right.
Together we bask in the funny sight,
As friends gather close, hearts light up with delight.

Twilight's Embrace

As the sun dips low with a lazy grin,
Squirrels dance like they own the inn.
Neighbors peek out with a curious stare,
Wondering which cat will strut to declare.

Fireflies buzz with a flickering light,
Debating if they're quite ready for flight.
Chairs creak softly under weighty news,
Who left the grill on? Oh, it's just the snooze.

Lawn chairs claim tales of unplanned fun,
As burgers sizzle, one, two, then run.
A kid chases shadows, boots full of mud,
While adults sip tea, taking stock of the flood.

Twilight whispers secrets beneath a tree,
Ghosts of old pranks giggle with glee.
Who spilled the drinks? Who searched for the cat?
In this gentle chaos, we all tip our hat.

Illuminated Paths

The street lamps shine with an orange glow,
Drawing out crickets for their nightly show.
A dog barks loud, claiming the night,
While raccoons find snacks that seem just right.

Kids on their bikes ride like the wind,
Catching the flavor of chaos unpinned.
Sidewalks are stages, where laughter rings true,
As neighbors get caught in the whirlwind too.

The ice cream truck's jingle breaks through the air,
Children chase dreams without a care.
Flavors galore swirl in a cone,
Just please, no more sprinkles—we're already prone!

Under streetlights, friendships ignite,
Playing tag keeps shadows in sight.
Tonight's just a hiccup in time's endless lane,
With giggles and memories to treasure, not feign.

Flickers of Belonging

A porch swing creaks with tales of the past,
Sharing secrets only the night can cast.
Out come the stories, wild and absurd,
Like how Aunt June's cat once flag-waved a bird.

The moon winks down, a silver-eyed guide,
As family feuds often take a wild ride.
"Who brought the potato salad?" chimes with a cheer,
"Not again!" echoes laughter fueled by good beer.

Each flickering bulb seems to giggle and sway,
As shadows chase dreams that dance far away.
Someone's misplaced the remote for the night,
"Who took my burger?" is met with delight.

So here we gather, mismatched but bright,
Under the stars, basking in light.
Love weaves our tales, round and round,
In moments like these, true joy is found.

Glimmers of Reassurance

The porch lights hum with a comforting glow,
Like grandpa's old stories, that ebb and flow.
Cupcakes are hidden in a clown-shaped box,
   Just one more bite—let the sweet detox.

A cat jumps high, on a dare to impress,
While kids laugh hard—oh, what a mess!
Popsicles drip down sticky little hands,
As everyone schemes in whimsical plans.

One slight miscue leads to a pea-flinging war,
"Did you just throw that?" oh, yes, how it pours!
Laughter erupts, as the truce disappears,
We'll forever remember those foolish fears.

The night stretches on, full of giggles and fun,
As fireflies tease and the stars have begun.
In this quirky chaos, we gently agree,
This feeling of home is for you and for me.

Evening's Radiant Reassurance

As dusk unfolds, the glow appears,
It softly shimmers, calms our fears.
The worries fade, like socks once lost,
In laughter's light, we count the cost.

A moth flits by, in a dance so grand,
With eyes on it, we all take a stand.
"What's with the light?" one friend quips jest,
"Is it a beacon, or a flying pest?"

Each corner chuckles, shadows play,
We share our snacks, the night won't sway.
The echoes of joy, they bounce and soar,
While the moon checks in, peeking through the door.

So here we sit, with smiles so bright,
Content in our haven, a feast of delight.
Each glowing moment, a spark of cheer,
With every chuckle, we hold it near.

The Invitation of Gentle Light

In the dimming glow, fun invitations,
A call to gather, with silly elations.
"Who brought the chips?" someone exclaims wide,
The laughter bubbles like a new rollercoaster ride.

We trade our stories with a wink and a nod,
Imagining ghosts, and how they're a fraud.
"Oh, look at that!" someone points in glee,
A shadow that makes us feel oh-so-free.

The light plays tricks, and shadows become,
The strumming of laughter, our heartbeats hum.
Starlight chimes in, "Are we all just fools?
When the best of company is found in our schools?"

Should the winds howl or the clouds try to hide,
We'd still find joy, with friends by our side.
So, raise a glass to the times we've spent,
As the gentle light wraps us, and our hearts get bent.

With a Lightly Beating Heart

With a flicker of light, our secrets unfold,
The shadows listen, but never get bold.
"Did you hear that?" someone whispers with dread,
But a giggle erupts, and all worries are shed.

The chair squeaks loudly, the table wobbles too,
A crew of misfits, more fun than a zoo.
With marshmallows ready, and stories anew,
Each poke of the fire brings sparkles in view.

One friend proposes, "Let's roast this old shoe!"
And all feign horror, "But what would we chew?"
Our laughter erupts like a bubbling stew,
With light beating softly, we thrive in the crew.

So here's to the breeze, the crackles of night,
With hearts that are dancing, oh what a sight!
We'll cherish each giggle, hold them so tight,
In the snicker of shadows, all feels so right.

A Glow of Friendship's Vigil

When evening comes, our spirits ignite,
With flickering candles and laughter in sight.
The porch becomes home, the world fades away,
As we swap our stories, come what may.

With popcorn in hand and tales from the past,
Each chuckle erupts, how long can we last?
In the glow of the night, our hearts all align,
As friendship wraps 'round, it feels so divine.

We whisper of dreams, plot schemes for the morrow,
Dressed in our pjs, dismissing all sorrow.
The clock starts to giggle, "Just five more minutes!"
But we can't stop the fun; the night's our trinket!

So let's raise a toast, to the glow we've spun,
To the light of our laughter, it's only begun.
For in every shadow, there's joy to share,
In this glow of goodwill, we banish despair.

Flickering Faith

A lightbulb dances, won't you see?
It flickers like a bee on spree.
A moth bumps in, then flies away,
I swear it's playing hide and play.

The glow it gives is quite a tease,
Keeps me guessing, if you please.
Like making toast, it's either burnt,
Or perfect, but the night has turned.

In shadows cast, it jokes aloud,
A comedy of light, so proud.
It flicks and flutters just for fun,
As if it's training for a pun.

So here I sit, with snacks in hand,
Watching this light, a show so grand.
If faith can flicker, then I'll cheer,
For every laugh, there goes a tear!

Hearthside Reflections

By the fire, we share our dreams,
With marshmallows and silly schemes.
Our laughter echoes, warmth ignites,
As shadows dance in the cozy nights.

The cat jumps up on Grandma's lap,
As if to join our goofy chap.
He yawns, a king upon his throne,
While we tell tales of love we've known.

The crackling wood, a soothing sound,
We find our joy, our hugs rebound.
Each silly joke brings tears of mirth,
A hearthside chat, a treasure's worth.

The snacks are gone, what's left to share?
A glimpse of life, beyond compare.
We close our eyes, the tales don't stop,
In a world of laughter, we'll always drop!

Echoes of Warmth

In the night, where giggles sway,
Echoes ring, come what may.
A bumper car, an old joke told,
As warmth spills out, a tapestry gold.

The echo of laughter fills the air,
Even the moon can't help but stare.
As stars twinkle, we joke and jest,
In this warmth, our hearts find rest.

The shadows laugh along our side,
As if they too, in joy abide.
This clumsy dance, a merry plight,
Under the embrace of soft moonlight.

With every chuckle, another tale,
Filling our hearts like a ship's sail.
As echoes fade, the warmth won't cease,
In every laugh, we find our peace!

Landing in the Night

As night descends, our feet take flight,
Landing softly, oh what a sight!
With silly hats and goofy grins,
We stumble in, let the night begin!

We dance on toes like clumsy sprites,
In this wild world of whispered bites.
Each corner brings a new surprise,
With laughter twinkling in our eyes.

The crickets chirp a wacky tune,
As shadows twist beneath the moon.
With every slip, a laugh erupts,
In this night game, we are abrupt.

So here we are, a motley crew,
With silly laughter, nothing new.
As the stars smile, we're home tonight,
In this sweet chaos, pure delight!

The Hearth of Heartfelt Return

In the glow of evening's cheer,
We dance with socks, not quite here.
The cat has found a comfy spot,
While snacks are banished, oh, what a plot!

Grandpa's stories twist and twine,
With odd inventions, all divine.
The fish that got away from him,
Grew to a whale, quite a whim!

Mom's casserole, a vibrant hue,
Creates a smell, but let's be true,
The smoke alarm sings out its tune,
Like a band that forgot the afternoon!

So here's to laughter, love, and fun,
Where joy and silliness are never done.
We raise a glass to the sweet absurd,
And toast to memories, the best word!

A Lighted Glimpse of Tomorrow

The lights are flickering, what a sight,
As I trip over cords in the soft night.
A brush with fate, a tumble, and roll,
As laughter erupts from my very soul!

The neighbor's dog thinks it's a race,
Chasing shadows with goofy grace.
I shout, 'Surely that dog can't fly!'
But then he leaps, and oh my, oh my!

In dreams we weave our silliest designs,
With bubble gum trees and candy lines.
Tomorrow may bring the same old grind,
But tonight, dear friend, let's unwind!

The future's bright, just like our feast,
With every laugh, our joys increased.
So let's light the way with a twinkle of cheer,
And dance in the glow until dawn draws near!

Embracing the Night's Kindness

Nightfall lingers with a silly grin,
As the moon plays tricks, let the fun begin.
We stargaze patterns, the owl gives a hoot,
While shadows bring giggles and silly pursuit.

The wind whispers tales, pure mischief and glee,
Of a time when my roast nearly flew from the spree.
My dog wagged his tail, joining the fun,
Chasing that turkey—oh, what a run!

Out in the dark, our laughter rings loud,
With brightly lit dreams, we're lost in a crowd.
The stars twinkle cheekily, winking their light,
Encouraging follies from dusk until night.

So let's raise a toast to quirky delight,
When mischief and magic unite in the night.
We embrace these moments, let nothing compare,
To the laughter and warmth we all gladly share!

The Radiant Echo of Homecoming

Homeward we wander, through the sweet breeze,
Where echoes of laughter float with such ease.
A pot of mischief, a tale to retell,
Of the time dad danced—oh, how we fell!

The door creaks open, a woeful squeak,
As mom finds the cat plotting her sneak.
Who snuck the treats? The evidence shows,
The furry suspect, in mischief, he grows!

Our stories collide, with giggles and grins,
As the night spins tales of losses and wins.
With each wacky joke, we've staked our claim,
In the heart of the home, that feels like a game.

So gather around, let the evening unfold,
As we bask in the warmth that never grows old.
To homecoming nights, with hearts full of cheer,
We celebrate joy, love, and a little bit of beer!

www.ingramcontent.com/pod-product-compliance
Lightning Source LLC
Chambersburg PA
CBHW060134230426
43661CB00003B/421